HELICOPTERS AND AIRPLANES
OF THE U.S. ARMY

Helicopters and Airplanes
of the U.S. Army

FRANK J. DELEAR

ILLUSTRATED WITH PHOTOGRAPHS

DODD, MEAD & COMPANY · NEW YORK

PICTURE CREDITS

Beech Aircraft Corporation, 39, 40, 41, 42, 43, 44, 45, 54, 55, 72, 73, 74; Bell Helicopter Company, 25, 27, 28, 29, 66, 67, 68, 70, 71; Boeing Company, Vertol Division, 2 (bottom), 46, 47, 48, 49; Cessna Aircraft Company, Commercial Aircraft Division, 75, 76, 77, 78; Connecticut Aeronautical Historical Association, Milton Sherman Collection, 14 (top), 15 (bottom), 20 (top), Percival Spencer Collection, 12; The de Havilland Aircraft of Canada Limited, 2 (top), 30, 31, 33, 34, 35, 36, 37, 38, 56, 57, 58, 59; The Grumman Corporation, 60, 61, 62; Hughes Helicopters, Division of Summa Corporation, 64, 84, 89, 90, 91; Hughes Tool Company, Aircraft Division, 65, 79, 81; *Jane's All the World's Aircraft* Photo, 13; Pratt & Whitney Aircraft, 8, 14 (bottom), 16, 20 (bottom), 21 (bottom), 22, 23, 24; Sikorsky Aircraft, Division of United Technologies, 19, 50, 51, 52, 53, 83, 86, 87, 88; U.S. Air Force Photos, 11, 21 (top); U.S. Army Photos, 10, 15 (top), 17, 18.

Frontispiece: **The CV-2 Caribou cargo plane (top) and the CH-47 Chinook helicopter.**

2 3 4 5 6 7 8 9 10

Library of Congress Cataloging in Publication Data

Delear, Frank J
 Helicopters and airplanes of the U. S. Army.

 SUMMARY: Gives a background of Army aviation and describes the purpose of the various types of aircraft used.
 1. Airplanes, Military—Juvenile literature. 2. Military helicopters—Juvenile literature. 3. United States. Army—Aviation—Juvenile literature. [1. Airplanes, Military. 2. United States. Army—Aviation]
I. Title.
UG1243.D44 358.4'18'3 77-6495
ISBN 0–396–07476–6

Acknowledgments

Grateful recognition is given to Col. Alexander J. Rankin, U.S. Army (Ret.), for his assistance and guidance in the preparation of this book. Recognition is also given to Lt. Col. William Duerre, public information officer, U.S. Army Aviation Center, Fort Rucker, Alabama, and to the public relations staffs of the aircraft manufacturers whose products are described in this book. And appreciation, also, to Marilyn Vissar for her painstaking and patient typing assistance.

This book is dedicated to the U.S. Army leaders, past and present, whose vision prompted the founding and fostering of Army Aviation, and to the Army aviators and crewmen who brought that vision to practical reality.

BOOKS BY FRANK J. DELEAR

IGOR SIKORSKY: HIS THREE CAREERS IN AVIATION

THE NEW WORLD OF HELICOPTERS

CONTENTS

The Douglas C-47, a part of Army Aviation heritage, was the most widely used military transport of all time. Power was from two Pratt & Whitney Twin Wasp engines.

Introduction / WHY ARMY AVIATION?

Why Army Aviation? Isn't the Army supposed to stay on the ground? What are soldiers doing up in the air? Those are fair questions which this book will answer.

First, the Army needs aircraft for much the same reasons it once needed horses and hilltops, and later trucks, jeeps, ambulances, artillery, and tethered observation balloons: to enable the soldier to move about and communicate on the battlefield; to help speed the wounded to medical aid; to learn more about the enemy's strength, whereabouts, and when and where he might strike; and to *strike him* quicker and with greater surprise.

With aircraft, the big difference is that the Army can do these jobs much faster and more effectively than in earlier days. As wheels replaced horses, so, to a large degree, wings have replaced wheels. As a result, Army aircraft now support the ground commander by performing all five functions of land combat: firing guns and artillery (firepower); maneuvering about on the battlefield (mobility); giving commands and directing the troops (command and control); learning as much as possible about the enemy (intelligence); and bringing supplies to the combat areas (logistics).

The concept of taking to the air to perform all five of those vital functions was introduced in the early 1960s and is called *organic airmobility*. That is, the aircraft are a basic, or organic, part of the ground forces—not something separate to be called upon only occasionally. The helicopters and airplanes of today's Army are designed to carry out the objectives of that concept.

Army Aviation is a heavy-duty, short-range kind of flying to which supersonic jets and spacecraft remain as remote as Mars. As one soldier said, "We can't all go to the moon; some must stay behind and fly low and slow." Low, yes, but fast indeed when compared with trucks, jeeps, artillery convoys, and marching troops.

Nuclear weapons—the so-called "area" weapons—have changed the face of the battlefield. Under such a threat, it would be suicidal to gather large numbers of troops in any one place. So, today's Army consists of small, fast-moving units scattered 10, 25, or 50 miles apart. The gaps between these units bring problems to troops and vehicles traveling on the earth's surface: rivers with no bridges, swamps or jungles with no roads, ridges with no passes, lakes with no boats, and always the threat of ambush.

Only aircraft can carry soldiers and their equipment up and over the barriers that have halted armies since time began. As a result, today's airmobile troops can reach combat objectives in minutes instead of hours or days, and without having to fight or suffer surprise attacks along the way.

Army Aviation traces its heritage back to the Wright Brothers. In 1909 the Army bought a Wright "Flyer," a biplane which averaged 42 miles per hour in speed tests and cost $30,000. It was the first military airplane purchased by anyone in the world.

At that time the airplane was not considered a weapon system by itself, for the concept of air power had hardly been considered. Rather, the airplane was considered to be a way of doing reconnaissance and observation much more quickly and thoroughly than by ground means. For example, the Army's first pilots were taught by the Wright Brothers at College Park in Maryland. The airplane was sent to Fort Sam Houston in Texas to be used by the Army in pursuing Mexican bandits who were raiding the border counties along the Rio Grande.

The Army's first airplane, the Wright Model B "Flyer," was purchased in 1909.

America's first heavy bomber, the Army Air Corps Barling XNB-1, was built in 1923. Six 400-hp Liberty engines powered this night bombardment long-distance airplane.

This proved to be quite successful and the Army bought more airplanes and assigned them to the U.S. Army Signal Corps, which was responsible for communications and reporting information. In order to properly manage these new machines the Signal Corps organized an Air Service.

Meanwhile, other armies in Europe also bought airplanes, and when World War I started both the Allies and Germany were using them for reconnaissance, observation, and rapid communications. At first, all the pilots were very friendly and used to wave to each other as they passed in the air. However, as the war progressed, they began shooting at each other with pistols and rifles, and very quickly the airplanes were armed with machine guns. Next, large airplanes were bought which carried bombs. All this led to the

The Army's first medium bomber, the Martin NBS-1 night bombardment short-distance bomber. This photo, taken at the Hartford, Connecticut, Air Meet of 1924 at Brainard Field, shows a Standard training plane in foreground.

need for separate organizations such as the U.S. Army Air Corps. Some of these, like the Royal Air Force in England, became separate military forces. Others remained as part of the armies.

Between World War I and World War II, airplanes developed very rapidly, and although our Air Corps remained a part of the Army, the principle mission of our Air Corps became *strategic* rather than *tactical* in support of the Army. For this reason, the ground Army reverted to small, simple airplanes to continue the necessary observation, reconnaissance, and artillery spotting—the original reasons why the Army bought airplanes.

After World War II (in 1947) our Air Corps became a separate military department called the U.S. Air Force, while the Army continued to buy planes to perform specialized missions not suited to the Air Force and its very large, high-performance airplanes. Then, the Army (which had bought its first helicopter in 1943) began buying more copters. They proved to be so useful to the Army that today's Army aircraft fleet consists principally of helicopters, about 90 percent, and the Army's airplanes are used now mostly for special electronic observation missions and for VIP transportation. Although the Army's aircraft are, for the most part, quite small compared with those of the Air Force and Naval Aviation, the Army now has more aircraft than either of its sister services.

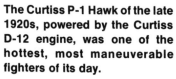

The Curtiss P-1 Hawk of the late 1920s, powered by the Curtiss D-12 engine, was one of the hottest, most maneuverable fighters of its day.

The Curtiss 0-11 Falcon of 1927, was standard Army observation aircraft in the late 1920s and early '30s.

In 1929, the Army Air Corps used the Pratt & Whitney-powered Keystone LB-7 Panther Bomber.

This Boeing XP-12A of 1929 was a prototype of one of the Army's most successful fighter planes.

The Army's first modern cantilever-wing fighter with retractable landing gear was the Seversky P-35 of 1936.

Boeing P-12E Army Air Corps fighters in formation flight in 1932.

Army Aviation, as it is known today, had its earliest beginnings in the spring of 1942 at Fort Sill, Oklahoma, with this group of 50 men and 19 Piper L-4 Cubs, also called Grasshoppers.

Army Aviation, as we know it today, was born on June 6, 1942, when the War Department approved aviation as a part of the field artillery, with the little Piper L-4 Cub being used as an artillery spotter. Fort Sill, Oklahoma, was the site of early flight training, but in 1954 the Army Aviation School was moved to Fort Rucker, Alabama. Today Fort Rucker is the location of the U.S. Army Aviation Center where the Army trains not only its own helicopter personnel, but other U.S. military and many foreign helicopter pilots and crews. At Rucker, the Army also develops advanced aircraft and equipment, together with new methods for using them.

The Piper Cub, also known as the Grasshopper, carried no bombs or weapons, yet packed a deadly punch. In just a few seconds, an L-4 spotter could call in by radio a destructive barrage on the enemy. The Cubs were not air power; rather, they added much to groundpower, for they were controlled by front line commanders who had their full-time use.

Piper L-4 Cubs, used as artillery spotters, are shown lined up at Fort Sill, Oklahoma, in 1942.

British Army fliers were the first to use light planes as artillery spotters. The U.S. Army quickly followed suit, first using L-4s as spotters in combat in North Africa in 1942. More than 5,000 of the slow, low-flying Grasshoppers were used by the Army during World War II. They played a big part in determining the outcome of the conflict.

The Army Air Corps also pioneered in the use of the helicopter, the amazing machine that lands and takes off vertically, hovers, and flies forward, sideward, and backward. In 1943, prodded by Capt. H. Franklin Gregory, a young man of vision and drive, the Corps bought the Sikorsky R-4, a little two-seat craft to be used as an observation-trainer. The R-4s were the only helicopters to serve in World War II. In 1944 one of them performed the first recorded rescue by helicopter—the pickup of three wounded British soldiers trapped behind enemy lines in Burma.

The Sikorsky R-4, the Army's first practical helicopter, entered service in 1943. R-4s were used in the China-Burma-India war theater and performed the first rescues of soldiers trapped behind enemy lines.

Above: In 1938, the Douglas B-18A bomber, powered by two Wright R-1820 Cyclone engines, was the standard medium bomber of the day. *Below:* Among the most famous airplanes in Army Aviation heritage was the Boeing B-17 Flying Fortress of World War II. It was powered by four Wright Cyclone engines.

Above: This North American B-25H Mitchell of 1943, an attack version of the B-25 medium bomber, carried a 75-mm cannon and was powered by two Wright R-2600 Cyclone engines of 1,700 hp each. *Below:* An outstanding long-range bomber of World War II, the Consolidated B-24 Liberator had four Pratt & Whitney Twin Wasp engines.

A high-speed, low-level attack plane, the Martin B-26 Marauder used two Pratt & Whitney Double Wasp engines of 2,000 hp each.

The Republic P-47 Thunderbolt, with its 2,000-hp Pratt & Whitney Double Wasp engine, was a leading high-altitude fighter of World War II.

The North American P-51 Mustang won fame in World War II as a long-range escort fighter. Packard-built Rolls-Royce Merlin engine provided the power.

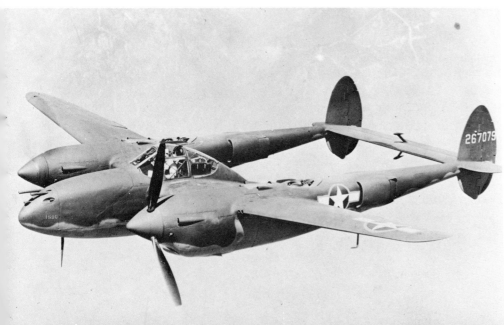

Lockheed's P-38 Lightning saw World War II fighter duty chiefly in the Pacific war theater. Two Allison V-1710 engines furnished the power.

Four-engined Douglas C-54 Skymaster later became the commercial DC-4 airliner. Engines were Pratt & Whitney R-2000 Twin Wasps. It served as a cargo and troop carrier.

Despite creation of the Air Force, the Army continued its operation of helicopters, using them chiefly as eyes for the ground forces. However, helicopters soon became the Army's strong arm (carrying supplies and equipment), its heart (evacuating the wounded to areas where they could receive prompt, lifesaving treatment), and its feet (enabling the foot soldier to move about with a speed he had never before known).

The helicopter first performed these services in combat in Korea. Medical evacuation (medevac) history was made in September, 1950, in a little village in western Korea, when three wounded American soldiers were flown to a field hospital. The men were strapped into pods fixed to the sides of the helicopter's fuselage. An Army chaplain who saw the helicopter take off recalled the scene years later.

"What a thrill it was to see that medevac by helicopter and to realize that here was something which was going to change the whole look of the battlefield," he said. "It is impossible to calculate the number of soldiers who survived in Korea and later in Vietnam because of the quick medical aid made possible by the helicopter.

"It used to take a half hour to get a wounded man to a first aid station, and as long as two or three days to get him to a field hospital. With the helicopter, a soldier could be in a field hospital within 15 to 30 minutes after suffering a wound."

It was at this time that a young Army doctor, Spurgeon Neel (now Major General Neel), first developed the now-famous MASH (Mobile Army Surgical Hospital), later the basis for a popular television series.

During the Vietnam war the Army developed its first full family of five helicopter types: troop carriers,

The Army used helicopters for medical evacuation (medevac) in Korea. Helicopter here is a Bell OH-13.

gunships, cargo transports, "flying cranes" for lifting heavy external loads, and observation aircraft. It was a long, tragic, and, in the end, a very unpopular war. Still, the Army did its best to handle the job assigned to it, calling upon its aircraft again and again to prevent difficult conditions from becoming impossible.

How has all this tradition, foresight, planning, and hard work in the field of aviation turned out for the U.S. Army? Probably the best way to find out is to examine the helicopters and airplanes of today's Army in the light of the jobs for which they were designed. This should show how they have performed, or are performing, their various tasks—how effectively they are helping the Army carry out its responsibilities to national defense.

Aircraft specifications and performance figures are given. In the case of helicopters, you will note hover ceilings given as OGE and IGE. The letters stand for "out of ground effect" and "in ground effect." OGE indicates the maximum altitude at which the helicopter can hover without being close enough to the ground to create a cushion of air that increases lift. IGE indicates the maximum altitude at which the helicopter can hover with the added aid of its own ground air cushion (for example, when it is operating high in the mountains).

We shall also look briefly into the future to see how the aerial lessons learned thus far may be applied to strengthening tomorrow's Army. Such an Army, whose very existence tends to discourage attack by would-be aggressors, may well be considered a vital means toward avoiding war.

Part One / UTILITY AIRCRAFT

BELL UH-1 "HUEY" SERIES   "Huey." That's one of the best-known words in the world of helicopters. Army troops coined the word from HU-1, which was an earlier Army designation for this utility helicopter. The HU-1 grew out of the H-40 which was originally designed in 1955 as the Army's first medical evacuation helicopter. That was why the Huey had such a wide cabin—so that stretchers could be placed crosswise in the cabin.

The Huey nickname stuck, even though the Army later changed the designation to UH-1 and gave the new copter the official name Iroquois, in line with its policy of naming its aircraft after Indian tribes.

The first production Huey, the UH-1A, entered service in 1959. Through the years, engine power and passenger capacity doubled, and the fifth and latest model, the UH-1H, carries an 11-man squad and a crew of two. As an ambulance it transports six patients.

First production Huey, the Army's UH-1A, entered service in June, 1959. Design changes eventually doubled the Huey's passenger capacity.

A new model, the UH-1B, which joined the Army in March, 1964, had an improved rotor system. The B and later C models were used chiefly in fire support missions.

Built by Bell Helicopter Company, Fort Worth, Texas, the UH-1H has a two-bladed main rotor, an aluminum alloy fuselage, and a skid-type landing gear. Its specifications are: top speed, 126 mph (202 kph); cruise speed, 106 mph (170 kph); range, 123 miles (198 km); payload, 4,700 pounds; hover ceiling, OGE, 1,100 feet; hover ceiling, IGE, 4,100 feet; service ceiling, 12,600 feet; rate of climb, 1,630 feet per minute; cargo space, 220 cubic feet; length, 40 feet, 8 inches; height, 13 feet, 7 inches; main rotor diameter, 48 feet, 3 inches; tail rotor diameter, 8 feet, 6 inches; empty weight, 4,800 pounds; gross weight, 9,500 pounds; fuel, 220 gallons; engine, 1,250-hp Avco-Lycoming T-53-L-13 shaft turbine.

The Army used thousands of Hueys in Vietnam where, for the first time, airborne troops were landed combat-ready in the middle of enemy territory. Huey transports flew high to avoid ground fire, while at the landing zones armed Hueys dived down to clear the way for the troops. Later, Huey ambulances sped the wounded to rear area hospitals. The attack completed, the transports returned to fly the troops back to their home bases, with jungle trails and enemy ambush far below.

The Air Force, Marines, and Navy also used Hueys in Vietnam and, like the Army and many foreign military services, continue to fly them. The Huey's commercial counterparts, the Bell 204, 205, and 212 series, are used by the oil, construction, and logging industries. A twin-engined 212, introduced in 1970, serves as an executive transport and as a utility workhorse for industry.

New helicopters using advanced technology (for higher performance) and sturdier construction (for better resistance to gunfire and crash landings) will soon be doing the Army's combat jobs. In what numbers will these faster, safer, and more efficient copters be built? Col. Alexander J. Rankin, who contributed much to the growth of Army Aviation, is optimistic.

"Past predictions about the expansion of Army Aviation, no matter how optimistic, have always turned out to be too conservative," he says. "So, I'm not at all hesitant to predict skies full of these new and better helicopters as the Army increasingly replaces its jeeps with air vehicles."

Left: The larger UH-1D tactical transport, designed to carry a complete squad of 11 men, entered Army service in 1963. **Right:** A more powerful engine in 1967 resulted in redesignation of the D model as the UH-1H. The combined production total of all military and civil versions of the Huey exceeds 12,000.

DE HAVILLAND UV-18A TWIN OTTER

Development of the lightweight PT6 turboprop engine by United Aircraft of Canada, Ltd. (now Pratt & Whitney Aircraft of Canada) led to a highly successful new airplane, the de Havilland DHC-6 Twin Otter, which first flew in May, 1965.

The new STOL (Short Takeoff and Landing) aircraft became an instant success, especially for commuter airlines in the United States. By 1976 it was used in 57 countries by 19 defense, police, and government agencies and 135 civilian operators.

In the early 1970s, the U.S. Army was seeking a transport for "command administrative, logistical and personnel flights from battalion headquarters to remote village sites throughout western and northern Alaska on a year-round basis." To meet that demand, the Twin Otter joined the Army in 1976 under the

The de Havilland UV-18A Twin Otter converts readily from wheels to wheel-skis, floats, or high-flotation tires.

Exceptional fuel economy enables the UV-18A to stay aloft for more than six hours on reconnaissance or search-and-rescue missions.

designation UV-18A. The choice was not surprising in view of the Army's long experience with the earlier de Havilland STOLs—the Beaver and Otter utility aircraft and the twin-engined Caribou and Buffalo troop and cargo transports. The UV-18A offered the Army several useful features:

It converts quickly from wheels to wheel-skis, floats, or high flotation tires, and the Army equipped its Twin Otters with all of them.

It carries 19 troops in and out of rough, makeshift airstrips 1,000 feet long, with room to spare. In 15 minutes two men can change it to a cargo plane that carries a payload of more than two tons.

On observation or search-and-rescue flights it can stay aloft for more than six hours because of the excellent fuel economy of its small turbine engines. It cruises at 195 mph (313 kph) at 10,000 feet and is easily controlled at 80 mph (129 kph) for accurate dropping of men and supplies by parachute.

The UV-18A is a twin-engined, high-wing, strut-braced monoplane of aluminum alloy construction and fixed (nonretractable) tricycle landing gear. An important design feature is its double-slotted flaps and ailerons which enable it to make slow, steep, landing descents, providing the pilots an excellent view of the landing area.

A few of the Twin Otter's vital statistics: takeoff run, 860 feet; landing run, 950 feet; takeoff run (STOL), 700 feet; landing run (STOL), 515 feet; stall speed with flaps, 66 mph (106 kph); rate of climb, 1,600 feet per minute; ceiling, 26,700 feet; cruise speed, sea level, 184 mph (296 kph); cruise speed, 10,000 feet, 201 mph (323 kph); range with 3,350-pound payload, 747 miles (1,202 km); range with 5,250-pound payload, 46 miles (74 km); range with wing tanks and 2,600-pound payload, 977 miles (1,573 km); maximum takeoff weight, 12,500 pounds; maximum landing weight, 12,300 pounds; span, 65 feet; length, 51.8 feet; height, 18.6 feet.

DE HAVILLAND U-6 BEAVER   Beaver is one of the great names in Canadian aviation. In 1946 Canadian officials began seeking a new bush plane to replace the pre-World War II and converted warplanes then operating in the Canadian northland. They distributed questionnaires to bush pilots from coast to coast. The result was the DHC-2 Beaver, which made its first test flight in August, 1947, and over the years became the all-time classic bush plane.

With a 20-mph headwind, the de Havilland U-6 Beaver can take off fully loaded in only 325 feet.

The Beaver could operate out of small fields and, as a seaplane, out of tiny lakes. It was the first STOL (Short Takeoff and Landing) plane to go into large-scale production. Political factors prevented its sales in the United States until 1951 when, in competition against six other types, it was selected as a U.S. Army liaison plane, the L-20. It later became the U-6 as its operations were expanded into general utility missions.

In Korea, the Beaver became known as the "General's Jeep" and was used by many U.S. senior officers to visit front line positions. It was chosen as the personal transport of President Eisenhower when he visited Korea in 1953.

De Havilland built 1,632 Beavers for civilian and military use. By the end of 1967, some 1,600 Beavers were in operation in 65 countries.

With a payload of seven passengers, or three-quarters of a ton of cargo, the Beaver becomes airborne after a run of less than 600 feet. Its excellent all-round performance is enhanced by one of the most dependable piston engines ever built, Pratt & Whitney's 450-hp R-985 Wasp, Jr.

The Army's use of the Beaver included:

By headquarters, as a command plane for rapid movement of commanders within battle areas.

By the Infantry, to speed the transportation of troops and supplies. In Korea, 50 Beavers, in four hours, moved an entire regiment across a mountain range, a job which would have taken Army trucks three days.

By the Signal Corps, for wire laying and courier services.

By Ordnance, for transporting and air-dropping supplies.

By the Medical corps, for evacuating the wounded and carrying medical supplies. In Korea, one Beaver alone carried 200 casualties from a front line battle zone during a three-week period.

The Beaver's specifications as a landplane include: top speed, 160 mph (257 kph); cruise speed, 130 mph (209 kph); maximum range at 5,000 feet, 650 miles (1,047 km), or, with long-range tanks, 945 miles (1,521 km); service ceiling, 18,000 feet; gross weight, 5,100 pounds; payload on 200-mile flight, 1,595 pounds; takeoff, full gross weight, no wind, 560 feet; landing roll, 500 feet; wing span, 48 feet; length, 30 feet, 4 inches; height, 9 feet; propeller, two-bladed Hamilton Standard Constant Speed; fuel, 95 gallons, plus 43 gallons in wing-tip tanks.

A sturdy, all-metal, high-wing monoplane, the Beaver was designed to operate on wheels, floats, skis, as an amphibian, or with the de Havilland wheel-ski combination—a truly versatile airplane able to operate anywhere in the world.

The Beaver was designed essentially as a seaplane. Its high wing permits easy mooring at docks and shorelines.

DE HAVILLAND U-1A OTTER

"An airborne one-ton truck." That's how the U-1A Otter is described in U.S. Army Aviation circles. The reference is to the Otter's payload of 2,100 pounds—just over one ton.

The Army has used the U-1A extensively for topographical survey in areas ranging from the icebound shores of the Alaskan Artic coastline to the Panama Canal Zone. Other Army missions for the Otter have included ambulance, liaison, communications, and transportation of passengers and supplies.

Army engineers found the sea plane version of the Otter especially useful in Alaska where the Otters landed on open rivers or lakes and, drawing only two feet of water, were able to taxi close to shore and unload supplies and replacements.

The Otter is excellent for parachute dropping of supplies and for paratrooper training because of the high position of its horizontal tail surfaces, easy removal of its left-hand loading doors, and steady control at low speeds. Drops can be made at speeds ranging from 60 to 140 mph (96 to 225 kph).

Built by de Havilland Aircraft of Canada, Ltd., Downsview, Ontario, the Otter was based on the success of the earlier one-half-ton payload Beaver. Like the Beaver, the Otter was flown with wheels, wheels and skis, skis, and floats, enabling it to operate from hard-surfaced runways, snow-covered fields,

Movement of supplies is one of many missions for the Otter, the Army's "airborne one-ton truck."

Excellent control at low speeds makes the de Havilland U-1A Otter ideal for the training of paratroopers.

and water. It can take off with a full load, in zero wind conditions, in only 630 feet. Thus, it can operate out of small fields, short jungle landing strips, or a stretch of road less than 1,000 feet long. This makes it a STOL, or Short Takeoff and Landing, aircraft. By providing added lift at low speeds, the Otter's full-span double-slotted flaps contribute much to the short takeoff and landing runs.

The Otter is an all-metal, high-wing monoplane powered by a Pratt & Whitney R-1340 Wasp engine of 600 hp, driving a three-bladed Hamilton Standard Hydromatic propeller. Its other vital statistics as a landplane are: wing span, 58 feet; length, 41 feet, 10 inches; gross weight, 8,000 pounds; fuel, 216 gallons; cruise speed, 138 mph (222 kph); top speed, 160 mph (258 kph); cruising range, 875 miles (1,409 km); service ceiling, 17,400 feet; endurance, 6.9 hours; rate of climb, 735 feet per minute.

Otters are used by several other military services and also as a civilian plane for airline, freight, exploration, and general utility missions around the world. Almost 500 were built before production ended in 1967.

Simple, rugged lines of the U-1A Otter are seen in this formation flight photo. As a cargo plane, the Otter has a 3,045-pound payload with fuel for 200 miles.

The first Seminole, U-8A, was derived from the Beechcraft 50 Twin Bonanza, widely used in civil aviation.

BEECH U-8 SEMINOLE
The U-8 Seminole is a high-performance, all-weather personnel transport and courier which is adaptable to pilot training or cargo hauling. The Seminole may also be quickly converted as an air evacuation ambulance to carry litter patients.

Four models of the U-8 have been produced for the Army—the U-8A, D, G, and F, with the last three still in use. Design and equipment changes through the years brought improved performance, especially in the load carrying and range of the later models. For example, the U-8F has a useful load of 2,588 pounds and a cruising range of 1,367 miles, compared to 1,483 pounds and 978 miles for the U-8A.

Manufactured by the Beech Aircraft Corporation of Wichita, Kansas, the U-8A, D, and G are derived from the civilian Beechcraft 50 Twin Bonanza, while the F model is a military version of the civilian Beechcraft 65 Queen Air. These sleek aircraft may be seen at almost any airport in the country, many thousands having been built for general aviation use.

39

The U-8F is an all-metal, low-wing monoplane with fully retractable tricycle landing gear. It has a maximum of seven seats, enabling it to carry five passengers and a crew of two. Power is provided by two Lycoming O-480-3 piston engines of 340 hp each, supercharged for high altitude flight and driving Hartzell three-bladed, all-metal propellers which can be fully feathered in case of engine failure.

Among the U-8F's other vital statistics: cruising speed at 10,000 feet, 200 mph (322 kph); top speed at 12,000 feet, 239 mph (385 kph); rate of climb at sea level, 1,300 feet per minute; service ceiling 27,000 feet; absolute ceiling, 28,500 feet; stalling speed, 80 mph (129 kph); takeoff distance, 1,180 feet; landing distance, 1,280 feet; cruising range at 10,000 feet and 184 mph (296 kph), 1,367 miles (2,201 km); endurance, 7.42 hours; empty weight, 5,112 pounds; useful load, 2,588 pounds; gross weight, 7,700 pounds; wing span, 45 feet, 10.4 inches; length, 33 feet, 4 inches; fuel capacity, 230 gallons.

With their high speed, long range, comfort, and adaptability to many tasks, U-8 Seminoles have played a major role for Army Aviation. Their assignment, with Army crews, to American embassies overseas, further indicates their popularity as utility aircraft.

Latest model, the U-8F, showed further design changes and a top speed of 239 mph (387 kph).

The U-8D Seminole has top speed of 232 mph (374 kph), supercharged, fuel-injection engines. It is derived from civilian Beechcraft 65 Queen Air.

BEECH U-21A UTE

BEECH U-21A UTE   Here is another Army version of a popular Beech civilian aircraft—the Beechcraft Model 65-A90-1C. The Army describes the U-21A Ute as "a cross between the King Air and Queen Air civil models."

The U-21A has very good capabilities for short takeoff and landing and can be operated into and out of unimproved fields. With space for ten soldiers and a crew of two, the Ute was purchased as a tactical transport airplane to provide support for combat units in the field, rather than as a general administration support aircraft such as the U-8 series.

The U-21A is an unpressurized, high-performance, all-weather utility transport. Its features include a spacious, comfortable cabin, a large cargo door, and seats that are readily removable to permit the Ute to be flown as an ambulance or cargo plane.

Larger, faster, and more powerful than the U-8, the U-21A can carry its full complement of 12 occupants 840 miles (1,352 kilometers) at a cruising speed of 248 mph (399 kph) at an altitude of 10,000

A combat area workhorse, the U-21A Ute operates from unprepared fields in its support of Army tactical units.

Opposite: **A high-performance, all-weather transport, the U-21A carries ten passengers and a crew of two, is adaptable for cargo and ambulance missions.**

feet. This includes fuel for starting, taxiing, climbing to 10,000 feet, and a 45-minute fuel reserve at the destination.

The U-21A is powered by two 550-hp PT-6A-20 shaft turbine engines built by Pratt & Whitney Aircraft Ltd. of Longueuil, Canada. The three-bladed Hartzell propellers are full-feathering and reversing, the latter feature providing much of the stopping force required for landing on short, unprepared fields. The landing gear is of the tricycle type and fully retractable.

Among the Ute's performance specifications: maximum speed, 259 mph (417 kph); rate of climb, sea level, 1,950 feet per minute; stalling speed, 90 mph (144 kph); takeoff distance, 1,630 feet; landing distance, 1,280 feet.

Other vital statistics: empty weight, 5,155 pounds; maximum useful load, 4,470 pounds; takeoff gross

Overhead view of the U-21A shows the Hartzell propellers in the full-feathered position.

Antennae sprout from wings and tail of this Beech RU-21E, a reconnaissance version of the U-21A Ute.

weight, 9,650 pounds; wing span, 45 feet, 10.5 inches; length, 35.5 feet; height to top of tail fin, 14.2 feet; fuel capacity, including wing tanks, 370 gallons.

Special mission versions of the Ute—RU-21D reconnaissance aircraft—were delivered to the Army in the early 1970s. The deliveries included both new aircraft and conversions of U-21s and totalled about 50 aircraft.

Part Two / CARGO AIRCRAFT

BOEING-VERTOL CH-47 CHINOOK   The CH-47 Chinook bears the designation "CH," for cargo helicopter, but there is scarcely an aerial job that this versatile aircraft has not done for the Army.

The Chinook is an air transport/crane-type vehicle that can perform many tasks beyond its primary role of supporting the ground forces. The list covers a large share of the jobs for which the Army has used rotorcraft: troop transport and supply, internal cargo, external cargo, rescue and evacuation, aircraft recovery, amphibious operations, ship-to-shore and shore-to-ship supply, and self-deployment.

A CH-47C Chinook lifts a 17,000-pound tractor at Fort Sill, Oklahoma.

Chinooks are used from the tropics to the Far North. Here, troops in arctic garb board a Chinook in Alaska.

Recovery of downed aircraft was one of the Chinook's unique achievements in Vietnam. From September, 1965, when they were first deployed in Southeast Asia, to the war's end, the Chinooks recovered more than 10,000 aircraft with a total estimated value of more than $3 billion.

Built by the Boeing Company, Vertol Division, of Morton, Pennsylvania, the Chinook was first delivered to the Army in 1962 as the CH-47A (13,800-pound payload). With the Army's need for increased performance, two other models followed—the CH-47B (19,300-pound payload) in 1967 and the CH-47C (23,100-pound payload) in 1968. The very latest version is the D model, which has more powerful engines and an uprated drive system to provide even greater payloads and higher speeds. It also has improvements in the rotor blades and in the hydraulic, electrical, flight control, and cargo suspension systems. The A, B, and C models are being returned from service to be modernized as D models, a step which is expected to extend the life of the Chinook into the 1990s.

More than 700 Chinooks were delivered to the U.S. Army. In addition, the C model is in operation with the armed forces of Australia, Iran, Italy, Spain, Canada, and Thailand.

Specifications of the new CH-47D: design gross weight, 33,000 pounds; maximum gross weight, 50,000

Left: A CH-47 Chinook airlifts three 500-gallon fuel cells. **Right:** Internal-external cargo-carrying ability enables a Chinook to transport a 155-mm howitzer, ammunition, and gun crew.

A Chinook hovers on a steep hillside while troops unload cargo from its rear ramp.

pounds; weight empty, 21,735 pounds; payload, 26,000 pounds (approx.); engines, two Avco-Lycoming T-55-11C turbines for total of 7,200 hp; top speed, 190 mph (306 kph); ferry range, 1,199 miles (1,930 km); forward rate of climb, 3,670 feet per minute; hover ceiling, OGE, 13,600 feet; range at 50,000 pounds gross weight, 320 miles (515 km); rotor diameter, 60 feet; length overall, blades extended, 99 feet; fuselage length, 51 feet; height, 18 feet, 7.8 inches.

SIKORSKY CH-54 TARHE

In 1963 the U.S. Army contracted to buy six Sikorsky S-64 Skycranes. Designated as the Army CH-54A Tarhe, this unusual "Flying Crane" helicopter with its beamlike fuselage carried a wide variety of external loads. In addition, it could be fitted with detachable vans, or pods, to accommodate troops or cargo, or to serve as field hospitals, command posts, and repair shops.

The Army accepted its first production CH-54As in June, 1964, flying four of the powerful new copters from the Sikorsky Aircraft plant, Stratford, Connecticut, to "Air Assault II," a major Army exercise held in the Carolinas. Performance of the Flying Cranes in those exercises provided a preview of what they were to accomplish in combat. The Cranes picked up airplanes as large as the CV-2 Caribou, carried 500-gallon

Van, or pod, fits neatly beneath Sikorsky CH-54A Flying Crane. Pods serve as command posts, field hospitals, and repair shops.

rubber fuel containers in clusters of four and five, and transported road graders, artillery pieces, and a 10-ton M-113 armored personnel carrier.

During the exercises a crane pod was converted into a tactical operations center for Maj. Gen. H. W. O. Kinnard and his staff. In Vietnam, little more than a year later, General Kinnard, as head of the Army's new First Cavalry Division (air mobile), was using a crane-transported pod as a command post.

The Flying Crane, using hooks and hoists to carry its cargoes externally, has no cabin except the pilots' compartment. One pilot's seat faces aft at a lower level than the forward-facing seats to provide the pilot a clear view of the cargo during pickups or deliveries.

In combat, the Flying Crane's jobs were many: carrying artillery batteries to a mountaintop, a bulldozer to a high ridge for construction of a radio relay station, damaged aircraft from land to ships offshore. Like the Chinook, the cranes recovered thousands of downed aircraft from enemy territory, again with savings that ran into billions of dollars.

The CH-54B holds nine world helicopter records—six for altitude and three for speed of climb. One climbing record found the big Crane rising 6,000 meters (19,685 feet) in only 2 minutes, 58.9 seconds. To appreciate the power and speed of that vertical ascent, at 10,000 feet the CH-54B would have been ahead

CH-54B Flying Crane, identified by its twin-tire main landing wheels, is built to get the job done, not to win beauty contests.

Flying Cranes, one carrying an Army pod, hover for the cameraman.

of an Apollo spacecraft on liftoff for a flight to the moon! On the same flight the copter reached 9,000 meters (29,527 feet) in only 5 minutes, 57.7 seconds.

To set one of the altitude marks, the Crane carried its maximum payload of 15,000 kilograms (33,075 pounds) to 10,850 feet, topping the record of the Russian V-12, a huge twin-rotor copter more than twice the size of the CH-54B. On another flight, without payload, the CH-54B set the record for altitude in horizontal flight, 36,122 feet.

The Army purchased 90 Flying Cranes, about 60 of the CH-54A model with a 10-ton payload, the balance being the CH-54B with a 12.5-ton payload. Specifications for the B model include: gross weight, 47,000 pounds; weight empty, 19,690 pounds; useful load, 27,310 pounds; engines, two Pratt & Whitney

JFTD12A-5A turbines of 4,800 hp each; length (blades extended), 88 feet, 6 inches; height (to top of tail rotor), 25 feet, 4 inches; main rotor diameter, 72 feet; tail rotor diameter, 16 feet; ground clearance below fuselage, 9 feet, 4 inches; cruise speed, 126 mph (203 kph); service ceiling at gross weight, 12,000 feet; best rate of climb, 8,300 feet per minute; hover ceiling OGE, 4,000 feet; hover ceiling, IGE, 7,200 feet; cockpit capacity, three pilots, two crew.

Commercially, the S-64 Skycrane is used chiefly in the heavy construction and logging industries.

Fitted with skis and auxiliary fuel tanks, Army CH-54Bs supported troops in Alaska, carried medipods with mobile clinics to remote villages.

Seventy C-12As are on order, 40 for the Army and 30 for the Air Force. They will be based at 32 locations in twenty-five countries.

BEECH C-12A
One of the Army's fastest and sleekest aircraft is the turboprop-powered C-12A, a pressurized, air-conditioned, fully instrumented transport whose basic mission is to speed passengers and cargo to any part of the world.

The C-12A (it has no official Army name, Indian or otherwise) is a military version of the T-tail Beechcraft Super King Air 200, introduced in 1974. The C-12A is also built for the U.S. Air Force.

As a personnel transport the C-12A accommodates eight passengers and a crew of two pilots, with ample luggage area and provisions for storing survival equipment. As a cargo plane it carries 2,000 pounds in its cabin area. The C-12A can operate under instrument flight conditions, day or night, into the world's major airports where air traffic is heaviest. Yet it can also operate from small, unimproved airfields.

Two Pratt & Whitney PT6A-38 turbine engines, of 750 hp each, driving three-bladed Hartzell propellers with full-feathering and reversing, give the C-12A a cruise speed of 256 mph (412 kph) and a range of 1,334 miles (2,148 km) at 30,000 feet. Its top speed, attained at an altitude of 14,000 feet, is 300 mph (483 kph). Pressurization provides a sea level cabin pressure at an altitude of 13,820 feet and a 9,350-foot cabin altitude pressure at 30,000 feet.

The Beechcraft King Air family of civilian and military turboprop airplanes numbers some 1,500, the largest number of turboprop aircraft ever built by a general aviation manufacturer. As a result, Beechcraft parts and service technicians are used in the worldwide support of the Army C-12As—a money-saving method in this special case. Generally, though, the Army uses its own equipment and mechanics to keep its aircraft flying.

Most of the C-12As bought so far by the Army and Air Force are assigned to U.S. embassies, attache offices, and military missions throughout the world. Their range, speed, payload, and economy save time and money in linking our nation's far-flung interests.

Army C-12A transport, an "off-the-shelf" version of the Beechcraft Super King Air, can speed passengers and cargo anywhere in the world.

DE HAVILLAND CV-2 CARIBOU

The de Havilland CV-2 Caribou (CV for cargo, short takeoff) is a military version of the DHC-4A Caribou which made its first flight in July, 1958. The DHC-4A introduced a new concept in transport aircraft design: a twin-engined passenger-cargo aircraft able to carry payloads up to four-and-a-quarter tons and yet able also to operate from short, unprepared airstrips. Like its predecessors, the Beaver and Otter, it is a STOL.

The U.S. Army bought five Caribous for evaluation late in 1957. The Army was so interested in the Caribou that a ruling limiting the Army to operation of aircraft weighing not over 5,000 pounds was set aside to permit purchase of the new transport. The Caribou became the third aircraft built by de Havilland of Canada to enter service with U.S. military services. More than 150 CV-2s were sold to the Army.

As an Army transport, the Caribou was designed to operate from short, improvised airstrips in close support of the troops in forward battle areas—carrying out aerial supply dropping, transportation of men and materials, and evacuation of the wounded. It transports 32 fully equipped troops, or, as an ambulance, 22 stretcher cases.

The Caribou's rear loading doors permit a three-ton truck to back up a ramp and into the cargo cabin. Jeeps can be easily driven in, while cargo can be quickly rolled into the cabin on roller conveyors. The doors can be opened in flight for delivery of supplies, or for dropping paratroopers or rescue crews.

Simple, all-metal construction of the de Havilland CV-2 Caribou provides low-cost service and maintenance.

The Caribou's short-field performance and low-speed control are based on de Havilland's experience with the Beaver and Otter.

As with all aircraft, the Caribou's payload varies greatly with the distance to be flown. For example, at a distance of 230 miles (370 km), the payload is 8,620 pounds, while at 1,092 miles (1,769 km), the payload drops to 5,417 pounds.

The Caribou's vital statistics include: maximum range, 1,391 miles (2,240 km); cruise speed at 7,500 feet, 182 mph (293 kph); service ceiling, 26,600 feet; absolute ceiling, 27,900 feet; takeoff run, 540 feet; landing run, 525 feet; stalling speed, 64 mph (103 kph); gross weight, 28,500 pounds; empty weight, 17,630 pounds; wing span, 95 feet, 7.5 inches; length, 72 feet, 7 inches; engines, two Pratt & Whitney R-2000 piston-type of 1,450 hp each; propellers, Hamilton Standard three-bladed 43D50, full-feathering; fuel, 829 gallons.

The Buffalo's T-tail aids STOL performance by reducing the aerodynamic effects of changing engine powers.

DE HAVILLAND CV-7 BUFFALO
The CV-7 Buffalo was designed to meet a military need for a larger, turbine-powered replacement for the CV-2 Caribou. The design goals were very severe: operation from grass strips 1,000 feet long and with 50-foot obstacles at each end, as well as operation from soft, rough surfaces.

The Buffalo (de Havilland DHC-5D) met its design goals and more. It has excellent STOL performance with payloads up to nine tons; steep climb after takeoff, and steep landing approach; good control and stability at low speeds, cruise speeds up to 287 mph (462 kph); a landing gear built for hard landings on rough fields, and a large rear-loading door for easy delivery of cargo both in air drops and on the ground.

The Buffalo's excellent short-field performance results chiefly from a simple high-lift wing system using double-slotted flaps to provide the steep, nose-down approach, and, after touchdown, wing-spoilers, powerful turboprop engines, and reversing propellers to bring the big transport to a quick stop after a roll of only about 500 feet.

As an Army tactical transport, the CV-7 uses its spacious cabin to carry 41 fully-equipped troops or 24 litter patients plus six seats, 18,000 pounds of cargo, various vehicles and weapons, and photographic and search-and-rescue equipment.

The Buffalo's performance varies widely, depending upon its specific mission. For example, as an assault STOL aircraft using short, unprepared airstrips, its best range is 402 miles (649 km) with a payload of 12,200 pounds. As a STOL transport using longer fields, the range increases to 690 miles (1,110 km) and the payload to 18,000 pounds (9 tons).

The Buffalo, which made its first flight in April, 1964, may be regarded as a compromise between high-speed, long-range transports requiring long, paved runways, and VTOL (Vertical Takeoff and Landing) aircraft able to hover and land at zero airspeed. Thus far the only production VTOLs are helicopters.

Additional CV-7 statistics (for the short-field STOL assault mission): maximum takeoff weight, 41,500 pounds; maximum landing weight, 39,100 pounds; weight empty, 24,800 pounds; takeoff over 50-foot obstacle, 1,190 feet; landing over 50-foot obstacle, 980 feet; rate of climb, 2,200 feet per minute; service ceiling, 31,500 feet; cruise speed at 10,000 feet, 287 mph (462 kph); fuel total, 2,107 gallons; range with zero payload at 10,000 feet, 2,035 miles (3,276 km); engines, General Electric CT64-820-4 turbines of 3,095 hp each; propellers, Hamilton Standard 63E60, three-bladed, feathering, reversing; wing span, 96 feet; length, 79 feet; height to top of T-tail, 28 feet, 8 inches; cabin length, 31 feet, 5 inches.

Long stroke landing gear of de Havilland CV-7 Buffalo withstands touchdowns of 13 feet per second descent.

Part Three / OBSERVATION AIRCRAFT

GRUMMAN OV-1 MOHAWK   There's an old saying, "You can't hit what you can't see." The OV-1 Mohawk helps the Army "see" in daylight, darkness, and in foggy weather. It does so with an array of electronic and photographic equipment which provides the field commander with information on the strength, location, and activity of enemy forces.

Built by The Grumman Corporation, of Bethpage, Long Island, New York, the Mohawk is a mid-wing monoplane powered by two turboprop engines. First received by the Army in 1960, the Mohawk has been produced in four models: the A which had one photographic system; the B which added Side-Looking Airborne Radar (SLAR); the C which had two photo systems and in which infrared cameras replaced the radar; and the D which has three photo systems and in which the equipment can be quickly interchanged (in about an hour) to perform the jobs of any previous Mohawk. These jobs are three: photographic, radar/photographic, and infrared/photographic.

In technical terms the OV-1D is "a completely integrated battlefield surveillance system." In simplest

Mohawks have served as surveillance systems in Europe, Korea, Southeast Asia, Alaska, and the United States.

terms, the OV-1D's varied equipment gives its crews photographic films and TV displays of the terrain and activity ahead of the airplane, under it, and to both sides. The infrared detects heat, such as campfires or boat engines, making it a good weapon against night guerrilla activity.

When the Mohawk enters enemy territory it flies at the lowest possible altitude, using hills and ridges to hide from enemy radar. Once in the target area, it pops up to a higher altitude, makes its observation surveillance run, and then dives back to the protection of the terrain. Its turbine engines and slow-turning propellers make it a very quiet aircraft, reducing further its exposure to enemy ground fire.

Like all Army aircraft, the Mohawk is designed to operate from small, unimproved fields. Its stall speed ranges from 63 mph (101 kph) for the OV-1C to 83 mph (133 kph) for the heavier OV-1D. Its "bugeye" cockpit canopy provides excellent visibility for its two-man crew.

Grumman OV-1D Mohawk flies at treetop levels to avoid enemy radar before zooming up to make a surveillance run of enemy territory.

OV-1B Mohawk carries antenna for side-looking radar in external case fitted beneath its fuselage.

Performance of the OV-1D for the infrared/photo mission: top speed at 10,000 feet, 305 mph (491 kph); stall speed, 83 mph (133 kph); takeoff over 50-foot obstacle, 1,145 feet; landing over 50-foot obstacle, 1,050 feet; rate of climb, 3,618 feet per minute; service ceiling, 25,000 feet; maximum endurance, at 161 mph (259 kph) at 15,000 feet, 4.5 hours; range at 20,000 feet, full fuel plus two 150-gallon external tanks, 1,010 miles (1,626 km); average speed at 1,010 range, 250 mph (403 kph); gross weight, 15,431 pounds; empty weight, 11,800 pounds; useful load, 3,631 pounds.

Further specifications: engines, two Avco-Lycoming T-53-L-701 of 1,400 hp each; propellers, two Hamilton Standard 53C51-27, full-feathering, reversing; fuel, 297 gallons internal, 300 gallons external; wing span, 52 feet; length, 41 feet; height, 12 feet, 8 inches.

HUGHES OH-6A CAYUSE

Twenty-three world helicopter records, including an amazing nonstop flight of 2,230 miles (3,590 kilometers), are among the achievements of the Army's light observation helicopter, the OH-6A Cayuse, built by Hughes Helicopters of Culver City, California.

When Hughes pilot Bob Ferry landed the little OH-6A on the sand of Ormond Beach, Florida, people gathered around and asked where he had come from. When he replied, "California," they said, "Where did you land last?" They could not believe that he had flown a helicopter such a distance nonstop and without refueling. But he had, and at an average speed of 140 mph (225 kph) and altitudes up to 24,000 feet. For this flight, Hughes won the Igor I. Sikorsky International Trophy awarded by the American Helicopter Society for the outstanding world record of 1967.

It was a remarkable feat for a single-engined helicopter with an empty weight of just over 1,200 pounds. What made it possible? Excellent overall design, skilled piloting, and, of course, extra fuel tanks inside the cabin.

The OH-6A was developed from the Hughes 369, a light, turbine-powered helicopter designed to compete with fixed-wing airplanes in speed, range, payload, and reliability. It won the Army's competition for a light observation helicopter (LOH) in 1964. With many new features, the OH-6A was designed from the start for commercial as well as military use. The Army ordered 1,071 in May, 1965, and eventually 1,434 Cayuses were delivered.

Flying at treetop levels in combat, the agile OH-6As performed command, control, observation, and reconnaissance missions, and proved able to sustain much damage and still return safely to base. The aircraft entered commercial service in 1969 as the Hughes 500, flying such missions as executive transport, cargo carrier, survey, patrol, photography, seeding, spraying, fire fighting, and air rescue, as well as doing many jobs for the construction, petroleum, and forestry industries.

In 1969, one OH-6A became known as the "world's quietest helicopter" through changes which included a five-bladed main rotor and four-bladed tail rotor (instead of four and two). These changes were later applied to Hughes' new commercial model, the 500D.

Specifications of the OH-6A: engine, Allison 250-018 turbine, 317 hp; maximum gross weight, 2,550 pounds; empty weight, 1,211 pounds; useful load, 1,339 pounds; top speed, 150 mph (242 kph); cruise

speed, 144 mph (232 kph); hover ceiling, OGE, 5,300 feet; hover ceiling, IGE, 8,200 feet; service ceiling, 14,500 feet; rate of climb, 1,700 feet per minute; range, 353 miles (568 km); endurance, 3.6 hours; capacity, pilot and three passengers; rotor system, four-bladed rotor, two-bladed tail rotor; rotor diameter, 24 feet, 4 inches; tail rotor, 4 feet, 2 inches; overall length, 30 feet, 4 inches; fuselage length, 23 feet; height, 8 feet, 6 inches.

In combat, the Cayuse was known for its agility and ability to survive damage from ground fire.

Opposite: **World-record, cross-country distance flight in 1967 demonstrated the OH-6A's excellence of design.**

BELL OH-58A KIOWA

In the late 1960s the Army asked the helicopter manufacturers to submit bids for follow-on production of a light observation helicopter (LOH). Hughes, as we have seen, had won the original LOH competition in 1964 with its high-performance OH-6A Cayuse.

In the new bidding, Bell Helicopter Company, Fort Worth, Texas, submitted the lowest price and on March 8, 1968, was awarded a contract for 2,200 helicopters under the designation OH-58A Kiowa. (A commercial version, the 206A Jet Ranger, is widely used by business and industry.)

Deliveries of Kiowas took place between May, 1969, and August, 1973. On December 8, 1969, the Army disclosed that the first deployment of OH-58As to battle units in Vietnam had taken place. The new copters flew both observation and scout missions, often in partnership with Bell HueyCobra gunships, the Kiowas seeking out the enemy and the Cobras performing the firing role.

The turbine-powered OH-58A replaced the earlier, and smaller, Bell OH-13 Sioux and Hiller OH-23 helicopters and the Cessna 0-1 Bird Dog airplane, all powered by piston-type engines. Besides its primary

OH-58A at left carries externally mounted 7.62-mm minigun for the scout mission, while aircraft at right flies in the observation configuration.

Protection for crew and vital aircraft parts is provided in the OH-58A by ceramic/fiberglass composite material, steel armor plate, and self-sealing fuel and oil systems.

observation/scout missions, the OH-58A performs many secondary roles. It replaces ground vehicles and assists larger helicopters in such tasks as command and control, liaison-courier, medical evacuation (two stretchers can be installed in one minute), communications, battlefield resupply, survey and mapping, wire laying and flight training.

A feature of the Kiowa is its semirigid, two-bladed rotor which provides simplicity, ruggedness, better rotor blade efficiency (through an advanced airfoil section), and improved autorotation for safe landings in case of engine failure. (At its maximum gross weight of 3,000 pounds, the OH-58A descends at a rate of only 1,300 to 1,500 feet per minute without engine power and touches down at zero airspeed.

For its observation mission the Kiowa shows these performance figures: maximum speed, 138 mph (222 kph); cruise speed, 115 mph (185 kph); range, 303 miles (488 km); rate of climb, 1,470 feet per minute; service ceiling, 13,300 feet; payload, 760 pounds; passengers (including pilot), four. The figures are reduced somewhat for the scout mission, which requires that the OH-58A carry a "minigun" machine gun and ammunition, and so must fly at a heavier weight.

The Kiowa's physical facts include: length, 40 feet, 4 inches; rotor diameter, 35 feet, 4 inches; height, 9 feet, 7 inches; empty weight, 1,586 pounds; gross weight, 3,000 pounds; fuel, 73 gallons; engine, one Allison T-63-A-700 turbine of 317 hp; armament, one pod-mounted 7.62-mm machine gun (minigun).

The Kiowa is designed to operate far from its home base, supported by one mechanic using a simple tool of the kind used by most garage mechanics.

Part Four / ATTACK AIRCRAFT

BELL AH-1G HUEYCOBRA   Here is another Army aircraft without an Indian name. When the Bell Helicopter Company developed the sleek new gunship in 1964 and '65, it sought a name to reflect the new copter's speed and firepower.

The Huey portion came from the fact that the new aircraft was a product improvement of the UH-1B which had been used with only moderate success as a gunship in Southeast Asia. Cobra was chosen as the tag end of the name because of that reptile's quick striking bite which is usually fatal. The Army agreed and gave its approval of the name.

The HueyCobra was developed because operations in Vietnam showed a need for a helicopter gunship with more speed, firepower, and maneuverability than the UH-1B. There was also a need for a gunship that could quickly be placed in production and easily fitted into the Army's helicopter fleet. The Cobra answered these requirements, and in April, 1966, the Army ordered 110 AH-1Gs, receiving the first one in June, 1967. By that fall, HueyCobras were seeing action in Vietnam.

The world's first helicopter to receive the attack (AH) designation, the AH-1G featured a new "door hinge" rotor which gave improved maneuverability and some increase in speed. To achieve the even higher speeds required, Bell had returned to its earlier concept of tandem seating of the two-man crew. (The pilot sits behind the co-pilot, who is also the gunner.) The tandem arrangement had been successfully tried in 1964 in Bell's experimental armed helicopter, the model 207 Sioux Scout. As a result, the HueyCobra's fuselage was only 36 inches wide, compared to the 100-inch wide cabin of the UH-1B.

Adding further to the speed was a 1,400-hp Avco-Lycoming T-53-L-13 turbine engine which, combined with the new rotor, gave about 200 more horsepower than the L-11 engine used in the UH-1B. In October, 1965, the HueyCobra reached speeds of almost 200 mph (322 kph) in level flight.

In all, Bell has built more than 1,300 AH-type helicopters, including more than 1,100 AH-1Gs for the Army. The balance went to the U.S. Marine Corps and the Iranian government under the designation AH-1J SeaCobra. In addition, improvements on the HueyCobra and SeaCobra brought further orders,

Tandem seating arrangement is shown in this view of the AH-1G HueyCobra helicopter gunship. A 7.62-mm minigun is on "chin" turret under the nose.

both for modification of older models and production of new ones. For example, 290 AH-1Gs were modified to carry the Army's anti-armor missile system known as TOW (for Tube-launched, Optically-tracked, Wire-guided missile).

Specifications for the AH-1G: gross weight, 9,500 pounds; maximum speed, 190 mph (306 kph); cruise speed, 150 mph (242 kph); range, 175 miles (280 km); armament, 7.62-mm miniguns, 2.75-inch rockets, and 40-mm grenades; length, 44 feet, 5 inches; height, 12 feet; rotor diameter, 44 feet; engine, Avco-Lycoming T-53-L-13 turbine, 1,400 hp.

Pencil-like lines of the AH-1G
HueyCobra account for its high
speed. Cabin is only 36 inches
wide.

Part Five / TRAINING AIRCRAFT

BEECHCRAFT T-42A BARON   Since 1965 most young Army helicopter and airplane pilots who have been transferred to assignments requiring them to fly twin-engined airplanes or to use instrument flight ratings have received their training in the T-42A, military counterpart of the Beechcraft B55 Baron.

The twin-engined T-42A has two training missions: First, instrument flight training, and second, twin-engine training of pilots who already have single-engine ratings. For the first half dozen years this training took place at the U.S. Army Aviation Center and School, Fort Rucker, Alabama, but later was dispersed to other Army airfields as training requirements grew with the Vietnam conflict. With the end of the war, training was again concentrated at Rucker.

Probably no other Army aircraft was put to such continuous use as the T-42A. The training flights went on, dawn to dusk, at an average of six flying hours a day, five days a week, year after year, with interruptions only for maintenance or serious weather conditions. "The engines never cool," the maintenance crews said, "unless the aircraft are in for servicing."

The Army is especially proud of one T-42A achievement—the plane's excellent safety record, which was gained despite a great number of takeoffs and landings and the meager experience of many of the

During engine warm-up before takeoff, crew reads through the checklist, stressed by the Army as vital to flight safety.

T-42As fly formation on a training flight. Army's flight safety programs have helped give the T-42A its excellent safety record.

flight students. One reason for this fine record is the Army's safety program, especially the use of a checklist before every flight. This list requires the crew to check every item critical to the proper operation of the plane—wing flap angle, engine power setting, free operation of all flight controls, and many others.

The training safety program also includes use of crash helmets for all crewmen, regular safety meetings for analyzing accidents, safety awards, and frequent aircraft inspections to look for safety problems.

"But it all goes back to the checklist," one safety officer said. "If a pilot does the same thing every time, there is very little chance to flip the landing gear handle instead of the flap handle, fail to check his fuel supply, or neglect any other flight procedure."

Army pilots receive twin-engine and instrument flight training in the Beechcraft T-42A Baron.

Built by Beech Aircraft Corporation, Wichita, Kansas, the four-seat T-42A Baron has these specifications: maximum speed, sea level, 235 mph (378 kph); cruise speed at 10,000 feet, 218 mph (351 kph); service ceiling, 19,700 feet; range, 1,225 miles (1,972 km); endurance, 7.5 hours; rate of climb, 1,670 feet per minute; engines, two Continental I00470-L piston-type, 260 hp each; propellers, McCauley two-bladed, full-feathering; wing span, 37 feet, 10 inches; length, 28 feet; height, 9 feet, 7 inches; weight empty, 3,197 pounds; gross weight, 5,100 pounds; seating, two crew, two passengers.

The Army received 55 T-42As as a result of a $2.5 million contract with Beech in 1965, and a year later ordered 10 more to bring the total fleet to 65. The T-42A was one of the first aircraft bought by the Army which was not designed as a combat operational aircraft. This means that the Army was able to buy it without the added cost of such protective devices as armor plate and self-sealing fuel tanks.

CESSNA T-41B MESCALERO

The T-41B Mescalero is the primary trainer used by U.S. Army fixed-wing pilots in their first weeks of flight training. Built by Cessna Aircraft Company, Wichita, Kansas, the T-41B is an "off-the-shelf" version of Cessna's widely used commercial model 172 which may be seen at almost any airport in the United States and a great many overseas.

The first six T-41Bs were received by the Army in November, 1966, and the final deliveries of the 255-plane, $4 million order were made in the spring of 1967.

For rough field operations, the aircraft had a minor design change—a heavier nose gear with a tire the same size as those on the main gear. The military interior of the four-place craft had shoulder harnesses for

The old and the new in training planes: Sleek Cessna T-41B Mescalero and the open-cockpit Stearman biplane of World War II vintage.

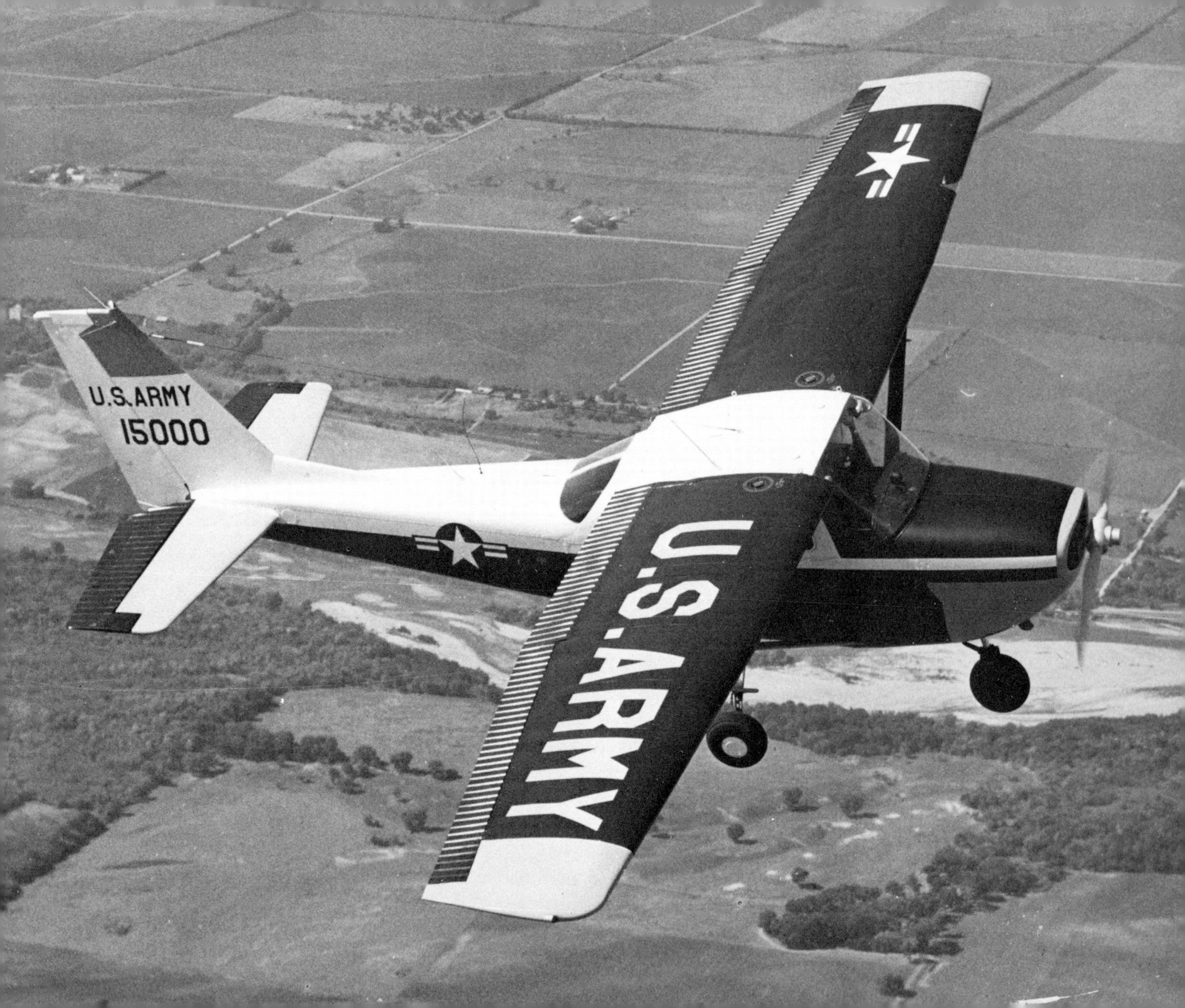
U.S.ARMY
15000
U.S.ARMY

Oversize nose wheel for rough field operations is seen in this view of the T-41B.

Opposite: Number 15000 on the tail section denotes this as the first of 255 Cessna T-41B trainers delivered to the Army.

the front seat occupants. Day-glo color (for easier spotting from the air in case of accident or forced landing) was used on upper sections of the wings and fuselage. Extensive navigation and communications equipment was installed, all vital to the training mission.

An all-metal, high-wing monoplane with fixed tricycle landing gear, the Mescalero is powered with a single Continental I0-360-D piston-type engine of 210 horsepower, driving a McCauley two-bladed constant-speed propeller. The T-41B's other statistics include: gross weight, 2,500 pounds; top speed at sea level, 153 mph (246 kph); cruise speed at 5,500 feet, 148 mph (248 kph); normal range (at 5,500 feet, 148 mph), 590 miles (950 km); maximum range (at 10,000 feet, 104 mph), 800 miles (1,288 km); rate of climb, 910 feet per minute; service ceiling, 17,500 feet; takeoff run on sod runway, 635 feet; takeoff over 50-foot obstacle, 1,045 feet; landing roll on sod runway, 400 feet; total landing run over 50-foot obstacle, 860 feet; empty weight, 1,550 pounds; wing loading, 14.3 pounds per sq. ft.; power loading, 11.9 pounds per hp; fuel capacity, 52 gallons.

The last three T-41B trainers of a $4 million order from the Army before their flyaway to Fort Ord, California.

Army T-41Bs, bought "off-the-shelf," are shown in production at Cessna Aircraft's plant at Wichita, Kansas.

HUGHES TH-55A OSAGE

Since the mid-1960s, Army fliers have enjoyed their introduction to the rotary-winged world by way of the Hughes TH-55A Osage, a peppy little two-place copter used as a primary trainer.

A military version of the Hughes 200 commercial helicopter, the TH-55A was bought "off-the-shelf" in July, 1964, following tests and evaluation by the Army. At that time, the 200, in production for almost three

Simple, compact design of the TH-55A is seen in this photograph of the Army's primary helicopter trainer in flight near the Hughes Aircraft plant, Culver City, California.

years, had logged 100,000 flight hours in the worldwide commercial and military applications and was adding to that total at a rate of about 1,000 flight hours daily.

In June of 1964, at the Hughes plant in Culver City, California, the 200 showed its simplicity of design and construction by setting a U.S. helicopter endurance record of 101 nonstop, nonmaintenance flight hours—equivalent to more than 6,300 flight miles (10,143 kilometers).

The TH-55A's buglike cabin provides unobstructed 360-degree visibility and has plenty of room for instructor and student. Other features vital to a good primary trainer are an 8-foot ground-to-rotor clearance for safe loading with the rotor turning; skid-type landing gear with special shock struts to absorb the impact of hard training landings; and low vibration and noise levels to keep student and instructor fatigue at a minimum.

Placement of the engine beneath the crew compartment, and the fuel tank in a safe position to the rear of the cabin, together with seats and fuselage structure designed to absorb crash impact, are intended to give the crew the best protection possible.

Performance and specifications of the TH-55A: maximum speed, 86 mph (138 kph); cruise speed, 81 mph (130 kph); endurance, 2.5 hours; hover ceiling, OGE, 4,000 feet; hover ceiling, IGE, 6,400 feet; gross weight, 1,600 pounds; empty weight, 1,010 pounds; useful load, 590 pounds; rate of climb, 1,350 feet per minute; engine, 4-cylinder Lycoming H10-360-B1A, 180 maximum hp; main rotor, 3 blades, 25.29-foot diameter; tail rotor, two blades, 3.33-foot diameter; length, 28 feet, 5 inches; height, 8 feet, 2 inches; seating, side-by-side, dual controls.

In all, Hughes delivered 860 TH-55As to the Army.

Readily accessible instruments, dual flight controls, and 360-degree visibility are among the cockpit features of the TH-55A.

Part Six / THE FUTURE

In time of peace the Army uses its airmobility in the public interest. This may be seen most notably with MAST—Military Assistance to Safety and Traffic—especially in the use of Army helicopters and aeromedical teams to speed assistance to civilians injured in motor vehicle accidents. Just as they once sped the wounded from battlefield to field hospitals, so are Army helicopters today speeding accident victims from highways to hospitals, thus saving hundreds of lives which would have been lost without such prompt attention.

Meanwhile, though, the Army's primary objective remains: be ready to meet any dangers to national security that fall within its field of responsibility. The dangers are quite real.

For example, in recent years new antiaircraft guns, surface-to-air missiles, and helicopter gunships have appeared in the hands of potential enemies of the United States.

Also, several European nations live under the threat of massive tank assault. The Army Aviation Center at Fort Rucker, Alabama, is studying this situation which, in Army terms, is called "the high-threat battlefield." Aviation, it has been decided, can do much to help reduce this threat.

First, the attack helicopter units with their HueyCobras are equipped to carry out their mission of finding and destroying tanks and other armored forces. The Cobras, now fitted with TOW missiles, can hit with good accuracy.

Second, the air cavalry has the airmobility needed to destroy attacking armored forces—day or night in almost any kind of weather. Training emphasizes "nap-of-the-earth" flying, which means flying at very low altitudes to take advantage of such natural concealment as valleys, hills, and trees. This type of flying, a natural for helicopters, hides the aircraft from enemy eyes and radar. Training also emphasizes night and instrument flying—both aimed at increasing the around-the-clock staying power of Army aircraft.

Finally, along with new training and tactics, the Army is developing a new fleet of aircraft for the future. These include:

• The UTTAS (Utility Tactical Transport Aircraft System), a vastly improved helicopter with all-new technology which will be the Army's first true squad carrier. Far superior to the Huey, it will also provide supply support and medical evacuation.

Sikorsky UTTAS helicopter has demonstrated bank angles in excess of 90 degrees and the agility needed for effective "nap-of-the-earth" operation.

On November 22, 1975, Hughes put both its YAH-64 prototypes for the AAH into the air. It was the first flight for aircraft number two.

• The AAH (Advanced Attack Helicopter), able to move quickly about the battlefield, selecting the time and place to attack enemy tanks and armor. Also based on new technology, the AAH is intended to replace the Cobra.

• The improved Chinook transport, mentioned earlier, which will fly faster and lower, carrying more troops, weapons, and supplies than its predecessor.

Of these three helicopters, the really new ones are the UTTAS and AAH. The Army selected them after the most intensive competitions ever conducted, competitions which had their beginnings in the early 1970s.

From a field of five companies, two were awarded development contracts to build UTTAS prototypes. They were Sikorsky Aircraft, Stratford, Connecticut, a division of United Technologies, and Boeing-Vertol, of Morton, Pennsylvania, a division of the Boeing Company. Each built three prototype helicopters which were turned over to the Army in early 1976 for exhaustive test and evaluation. On December 23, 1976, Sikorsky's entry, the YUH-60A, was declared the winner.

Competing for an AAH contract, and also selected from a field of five, were Hughes Helicopters of Culver City, California, a division of the Summa Corporation, and Bell Helicopter Textron, of Fort Worth, Texas. Each company built two experimental AAHs which competed in a fly-off for a development contract. (A production contract for the winner was to follow later.) On December 10, 1976, Hughes, with its YAH-64, was adjudged the winner, and awarded a $317.7 million engineering development contract for construction of three additional prototype aircraft as well as engineering development of various target, night-flying, and range-finding systems of the very latest design.

SIKORSKY UH-60A
When the Army opened the competition for a UTTAS helicopter it presented a list of requirements far more demanding than anything ever before asked of the helicopter manufacturers. Among the demands were:

• Hover out of ground effect at 4,000-foot altitude and 95 degrees temperature, and still have a vertical rate of climb of at least 450 feet per minute.

• Cruise at 167 mph (269 kph) or faster, while carrying 11 fully equipped troops and a crew of three for 2.3 hours.

• Have high maneuverability for safe "nap-of-the-earth" flying.

The Army demanded much more. The UTTAS had to be simply produced at low cost, easily maintained in the field, and be quickly loaded and carried in military transport planes. It had to be tough enough to withstand various gunfire hits and enable its occupants to survive the kinds of crashes which had demolished its predecessors.

The winner of the production contract, the Sikorsky UH-60A, showed that it could meet these demands during Government Competitive Tests (GCT) of three prototype YUH-60As flown by Army pilots. For

Unprecedented performance and minimum maintenance requirements of the Sikorsky UH-60A are the result of strict Army demands backed up by the latest design, material, and manufacturing developments.

example, it climbed vertically at 450 feet per minute at the critical Army conditions, using only 95 percent of power; cruised at 168 mph (270 kph), dashed at 189 mph (304 kph), and dived at 230 mph (373 kph). It also carried troops and crew the required 2.3 hours, maneuvered at loads of over 3 g's (three times the weight of gravity), and banked at angles as high as 100 degrees.

A great many design advances enable the new helicopter to outdo all previous helicopters. Included are new composite main rotor blades using titanium and fiber glass; elastomeric (layers of rubber and steel) bearings in the main rotor head, requiring no lubrication; a bearingless tail rotor needing no oil and grease; vibration absorbers in the main rotor system; a 48 percent reduction in the number of parts as compared with the earlier Sikorsky S-61 helicopter; and a landing gear and fuselage designed to enable crew and troops to survive a crash drop of 42 feet per second.

Other specifications of the UH-60A are: mission gross weight, 16,450 pounds; maximum gross weight, 20,250 pounds; hover ceiling, OGE, 10,400 feet; hover ceiling, IGE, 14,700 feet; service ceiling, 17,690 feet; two General Electric T-700 turboshaft engines.

How will the new UTTAS fit into the Army's future? Briefly, it is versatile enough to help in all five functions of Army combat, functions which were noted in the introduction to this book: mobility—the UH-60A will move a fully-equipped combat squad; firepower—this can be delivered from two gun doors; intelligence—long-range patrols, observers, and electronic sensors can be carried to hard-to-reach places; command and control—the UH-60A has the space, performance, and endurance to make an ideal mobile command headquarters; logistics—medical evacuation and resupply are among the natural missions for the UTTAS.

In March, 1976, a YUH-60A prototype flies over Connecticut en route from Sikorsky plant in Stratford to Bradley International Airport near Hartford. Three prototypes were delivered by Air Force C-141 transports.

The UH-60A lifts an Army vehicle weighing more than 7,000 pounds.

The UH-60A is a combat assault squad carrier designed to carry 11 fully equipped troops or up to 8,000 pounds external load in addition to the three-man crew.

HUGHES AH-64

Also aimed at the future and intended to do its share on the high-threat battlefield is the Hughes AH-64, an advanced attack helicopter designed to destroy enemy armored vehicles and to have the agility to survive in combat.

The war in Southeast Asia proved the helicopter to be a very special gunship for supporting ground troops. However, it also showed that the gunships then used were too easily knocked down by enemy ground fire. As a result, the Army, in 1972, asked the helicopter builders to come up with a new rotorcraft which would:

- Have enough gunpower to stop enemy tanks.
- Be tough enough to survive hits from explosive projectiles up to 23 millimeters in size.
- Be maneuverable enough to hide in the "nap-of-the-earth," yet fast enough to cover large areas of the battlefield.
- Be able to fly day or night and under adverse weather conditions.
- Be easily maintained in areas away from its base.

Hughes YAH-64 prototype in early test flight. Stub wing which mounts rockets and missiles, T-tail, and quiet tail rotor are among the new gunship's many design features.

Five 2.75-inch rockets streak toward target after launch from a Hughes YAH-64 prototype during test flight.

In addition to rockets, the AH-64 carries TOW antitank missiles and a "Chain Gun" cannon that fires up to 700 shots per minute.

The AH-64 is a lightweight helicopter of small overall size, weighing, when equipped for combat, almost a ton less than other helicopters designed for the same function. Despite its small size, there is ample crew space and weapon-carrying capacity.

The new attack helicopter carries TOW antitank missiles, 2.75-inch rockets, a 30-mm cannon, or a combination of these. The cannon, an XM-230 "Chain Gun" developed by the Hughes Ordnance Division, fires up to 700 shots per minute and is said to be one-half the size, weight, and cost of other such cannon. The "Chain Gun" is one more modern application of the well-known bicycle chain principal—a principal which was also used by the Wright Brothers to drive the propellers of their airplanes.

The AH-64 benefits from over two million combat flight hours with the Hughes OH-6A light observation helicopter (which was described earlier), since many of the attack helicopter's features are adapted from the smaller observation craft.

Among the AH-64's specifications: maximum speed, 191 mph (308 kph); cruise speed, 183 mph (295 kph); design speed limit, 235 mph (378 kph); rate of climb, 3,200 feet per minute; maximum range, 359 miles (578 km); ferry range (external fuel tanks), 1,167 miles (1,897 km); mission gross weight, 13,200 pounds; maximum gross weight, 17,500 pounds; service ceiling, 20,500 feet; hover ceiling, OGE, 11,800 feet; hover ceiling, IGE, 14,600 feet; power, two G.E. T-700 turboshaft engines; rotor system, four-bladed main rotor, four-bladed tail rotor; crew, pilot and co-pilot gunner, seated in tandem.

The Army plans to buy 536 of the new attack helicopters.

Both the UH-60A and the AH-64 are the result of years of Army planning, combined with the latest and best design innovations of the helicopter industry. The new helicopters also prove the wisdom of the Army's policy of selecting two top competitors for each new aircraft and then giving them a complete test and evaluation before choosing a winner. This is called "Fly before you buy."

This policy, supported by the Army's ever-growing wealth of aerial experience, bodes well for the future of Army Aviation and the nation's strength in this particular area of national security.

GLOSSARY OF GENERAL TERMS

AERODYNAMICS—Science dealing with motion of and forces acting on bodies moving through the air.

AERONAUTICS—Anything dealing with design, construction, and operation of aircraft.

AILERONS—Pairs of control surfaces on wings to provide rolling, or banking, motion to an airplane.

AIRDROP—Unloading of personnel or matériel from an aircraft in flight, usually in military operations.

AIR RECONNAISSANCE—Obtaining information by eyesight or by sensing equipment in an aircraft.

AIRFOIL—Any surface, such as a wing, designed to obtain reaction from the air through which it passes.

AIRSPEED—Speed of an aircraft in relation to the air.

ARMOR—Metal ceramics or composite materials used to protect crew or critical aircraft parts from enemy gunfire.

CAMBER—Curve of a wing section.

CEILING, ABSOLUTE—Altitude at which an aircraft's rate of climb is zero.

CEILING, SERVICE—Altitude at which an aircraft is unable to climb faster than a given rate (100 feet per minute in the U.S.)

CHECKLIST—List of operations to be checked by crew prior to takeoff or landing, to insure that nothing is overlooked or mishandled which would affect the safe operation of the aircraft.

CONTROLS—General term for any means to control the speed, direction, altitude, etc. of an aircraft.

DIVE—Steep descent in which airspeed is greater than the maximum possible in level flight.

ELEVATOR—Movable auxiliary airfoil to give pitching movement (nose up or down) to an aircraft.

FIN—Vertical fixed or adjustable airfoil to provide directional stability.

FLAP—Hinged or pivoted airfoil forming the rear part of wing to change the wing's camber (curve) and thus increase lift and drag for shorter takeoffs and landings.

FUEL TANK, AUXILIARY—A tank not a permanent part of the fuel system.

FUSELAGE—Body of an aircraft.

HORSEPOWER—Amount of energy needed to raise 550 pounds one foot in one second against the force of gravity.

LANDING GEAR, RETRACTABLE—Type of landing gear which may be withdrawn into the body or wings to reduce drag in flight.

LANDING RUN—Distance needed for an airplane to land, measured from point where wheels first touch ground to where plane stops.

LOADS—Useful load: crew, passengers, oil, and fuel. Payload: that part of the useful load from which money is derived (passengers and freight).

MILE, NAUTICAL—Unit for measuring distances at sea or in air. (One nautical mile equals 6,080.2 feet, or 1,853.25 meters.)

MILE, STATUTE—Unit for measuring distances on land. (One statute mile equals 5,280 feet.)

"OFF-THE-SHELF" PURCHASE—Aircraft bought with no major design changes (as a civilian aircraft type acquired for military use).

OVERALL LENGTH—Distance from extreme front to extreme rear of aircraft, including propeller and tail unit, and rotors for a helicopter.

POWER LOADING—Weight of an aircraft per one horsepower.

PROPELLER, CONSTANT SPEED—A propeller which runs at the same speed (revolutions per minute) despite changes in the airplane's speed, engine power, and altitude. Achieved by means of a device in the propeller hub which automatically controls the blade angles as conditions change.

PROPELLER, FEATHERING—Propeller whose blade angle may be lined up with the line of flight of the airplane, to reduce drag in case of engine failure.

PROPELLER, REVERSING—Propeller whose blade angle may be entirely reversed in flight; normally used to reduce the landing roll distance.

RANGE, MAXIMUM—Maximum distance an aircraft can cover at economical speed and altitude.

RATE OF CLIMB—Distance an aircraft climbs in one minute; usually stated in feet per minute.

RUDDER—Movable auxiliary airfoil to give a yawing (steering) motion to an aircraft (nose right or left).

SAFETY FACTOR—A design margin used to provide for the possibility of an aircraft encountering loads greater than expected in normal flight, and for uncertainties in design.

SLOT—Auxiliary airfoil at leading edge of wing to improve airflow and give more lift at steep angles of attack, as during takeoff and landing.

SPAN—Maximum distance tip to tip of a wing or airfoil.

SPOILER—Small movable plate to project above wing surface to disturb airflow and so reduce lift and increase drag; used to reduce speeds in dives or to reduce landing runs.

STABILITY—Property of an aircraft that, when its balance is disturbed, causes it to return to normal flight without use of controls.

STABILIZER—Fixed horizontal tail surface whose purpose is to increase the pitch stability of the aircraft.

STOL—Aircraft designed for short takeoff and landing, with minimum takeoff and landing roll, as an aircraft with wing flaps, slots, and other devices for very slow-speed flight.

TAKEOFF DISTANCE—Distance in which an airplane breaks contact with the ground or water, starting from zero speed.

VTOL—Aircraft designed for vertical takeoff and landing, with no takeoff or landing roll, as a helicopter or other direct-lift aircraft.

WEIGHT, GROSS—Total weight of aircraft fully loaded.

WING LOADING—Amount of weight of an aircraft that each square foot of wing area must lift.

GLOSSARY OF HELICOPTER TERMS

ADVANCING BLADE—The blade moving in the same direction as the helicopter.

ANTITORQUE ROTOR—The tail rotor, vertically mounted, which counteracts the torque or twisting effect of the main rotor; also provides directional control like the rudder on an airplane.

ARTICULATION—The hinging of the rotor blades to provide freedom of motion like a ball joint would.

AUTOGYRO—A type of rotorcraft whose lift is supplied chiefly from airfoils rotated by aerodynamic forces without direct application of engine power. Propulsion is provided by a propeller, as in an airplane. (Autogyros are not capable of true hovering, or of vertical takeoffs and landings.)

AUTOROTATION—The power-off, free-wheeling operation of a helicopter which provides a safe landing in event of engine failure.

BLADE LOADING—The gross weight of the helicopter divided by the total areas of the rotor blade outline.

BLADE TWIST—A twist built into the blade to reduce the lifting angle at the blade tip and increase the lifting angle inboard to improve lift efficiency.

COLLECTIVE PITCH CONTROL—The control which changes the pitch of all the blades simultaneously (for climb or descent).

CONTROL LAG—Time necessary for the rotor to reach a position in response to a control stick movement; in articulated rotors it is usually equal to the time required for one-fourth revolution of the rotor.

CONTROL STICK—Stick to control direction of flight (forward, rearward, or sideward) by changing the cyclic pitch of the blades.

CYCLIC CONTROL—Blade angle changes applied by the pilot to tilt the helicopter in the direction in which he wants to fly. (Less blade angle at the front and more at the back tilts the aircraft nose down for forward flight, for example.)

DISC AREA—The area of the outline of the rotor disc.

DISC LOADING—The gross weight of the helicopter divided by the area of the rotor disc.

FLAPPING—The up-and-down motion of rotor blades about the hinge at the blade root.

HELICOPTER—Any type of heavier-than-air craft which is lifted and supported in the air by surfaces or rotors turning on essentially vertical axes by means of power applied directly to the lifting surfaces.

HOVERING—Flight condition in which the helicopter does not move.

HOVERING, IN GROUND EFFECT (IGE)—Hovering close enough to the ground or water to compress a cushion of high density air between the main rotor and the ground or water, thus increasing the lift of the main rotor.

HOVERING, OUT OF GROUND EFFECT (OGE)—The opposite of the foregoing—not close enough to the ground to create cushion of air to increase lift.

IGE—See Hovering, in ground effect.

MAIN ROTOR—The main system of rotating blades, providing lift for the helicopter.

OGE—See Hovering, out of ground effect.

PITCH CONTROL—The mechanism that changes the rotor blade angle of attack, or pitch, usually divided into two controls—collective pitch and cyclic pitch control.

RETREATING BLADE—The rotor blade which is traveling in a direction opposite to that of the helicopter.

REVERSE FLOW REGION—That portion of the rotor disc in which the combined air flow is opposite to that of the remainder of the disc. (This occurs on the slower-moving inboard sections of a rotor blade at the higher forward speeds.)

ROTOR—A system of rotating airfoils, usually long, narrow, winglike structures, which provide the lift and thrust for a helicopter.

ROTOR BLADE CONING—The average angle between the blade span axis and the plane of the rotor disc. (The coning angle increases when a helicopter carries heavier loads.)

ROTOR DISC—The plane described by the path of the tips of the rotor blades.

ROTOR RPM—The rotational velocity of a rotor in revolutions per minute.

ROTOR TORQUE—The twisting movement required to turn a rotor.

ROTORCRAFT—Any aircraft deriving its principal lift from one or more rotors.

STABILITY—The property of a helicopter which tends to restore an original condition of steady flight after it has been disturbed by some external force, such as turbulent air.

STALLING OF BLADES—Condition of a rotor blade in which the streamline flow breaks down and the blade no longer produces increased lift for increase in angle of attack, and an increase in power is required.

TIP SPEED—The velocity of the outboard end of a rotor blade.

TRANSMISSION—A reduction gear unit linking the engine with the main rotor. The transmission has a free-wheeling unit to allow the rotor to continue rotation in case of engine failure.